T0198920

1 + 1 = 3

Conversation Guides for
Spiritual Mentorship

Alicia Marie Fay

WESTBOW
PRESS®
A DIVISION OF THOMAS NELSON
& ZONDERVAN

WestBow Press books may be ordered through booksellers or by contacting:

WestBow Press
A Division of Thomas Nelson & Zondervan
1663 Liberty Drive
Bloomington, IN 47403
www.westbowpress.com
1 (866) 928-1240

Because of the dynamic nature of the Internet, any web addresses or
links contained in this book may have changed since publication and
may no longer be valid. The views expressed in this work are solely those
of the author and do not necessarily reflect the views of the publisher,
and the publisher hereby disclaims any responsibility for them.

Any people depicted in stock imagery provided by Getty Images are
models, and such images are being used for illustrative purposes only.
Certain stock imagery © Getty Images.

Scripture taken from the NEW AMERICAN STANDARD BIBLE®,
Copyright © 1960, 1962, 1963, 1968, 1971, 1972, 1973, 1975, 1977,
1995 by The Lockman Foundation. Used by permission.

ISBN: 978-1-9736-8293-6 (sc)
ISBN: 978-1-9736-8295-0 (hc)
ISBN: 978-1-9736-8294-3 (e)

Library of Congress Control Number: 2020900324

Print information available on the last page.

WestBow Press rev. date: 01/16/2020

Contents

Introduction

As a self-employed writer and entrepreneur, almost nothing in my life requires me to wake up before about 9:00 a.m.—except every other Friday, when my alarm starts chirping at 6:15 a.m. And then I groggily drag myself out of bed and pour some coffee down my throat to coax my brain awake. On these mornings, yoga pants and sweatshirts are the norm, makeup is optional, and—yes—I've been known to leave wearing slippers, because very few things inspire me to be a morning person, but one thing can—my besties.

Karen, Jordan, and I met in seminary through a (mandatory) spiritual-development small group. We gathered together every week for two years, and over those years, we shared intimate details about our lives and hearts. We worked through many of the same questions that ultimately ended up in this book. In short, we set aside our natural fears of intimacy (yes, we all have them) and risked sharing our true selves.

As I write this, more than four years later, we still meet every other Friday. Even as some of us moved to different parts of the world, we still make time to video chat and share about our lives, our fears, and our big decisions and ask each other questions that no one else is willing to ask. I wouldn't trade these meetings, or these incredible ladies, for the world.

These are the kinds of relationships most of us deeply crave. They are the only kinds of relationships that can pry me out of bed in the early morning to drive across town and spend an hour sipping mediocre coffee in a restaurant booth. I don't go for the coffee. I don't even go for the conversation. I go for the *connection*. On good days or bad—in trials or victories—these are *my girls*. When I'm with them, I don't worry how I look or how stupid I sound when I talk. They love me either way. They hear me. They challenge me. They can be the voice of reason that quiets my chaos.

My dream is for everyone to experience relationships like these, but I know it isn't easy. Deep, authentic human connections don't happen automatically. Building "besties" requires a lot of intentionality, some patience, and a whole bucketload of courage. Even so, I firmly believe if we make a conscious choice to show up, share openly, and use some good tools (like this book) to guide us toward real honesty, then deep, authentic relationships do kind of just *happen*.

This book isn't a magic wand or secret formula; it's just a collection of conversation topics—but they work. These discussions meet us right in the middle of our complicated human issues and offer us a safer space to invite other human beings into our experiences. This is how relationships form. This is how people grow. It's time to let go of a tiny bit of the fear that is keeping you from opening your heart and take one brave step into real, honest, deep, life-changing friendship. I promise you won't regret it.

How 1 + 1 Can = 3

Where two or three have gathered together in My
name, I am there in their midst.
　　　　　　　　　　　—Matthew 18:20 (NASB)

God is present with us always, but something special happens when
two or more believers gather together in His name. I don't just read
about it in scripture; I see it happen in my own life and relationships.
When I invest in the life of another person, God shows up in unique
ways.

He multiplies the benefit of the time we spend together. He brings
wisdom and insight into our conversations that we didn't have before.
He provides comfort and encouragement in times of struggle. He
inspires joy and celebration more beautiful than we could experience
separately. We are creatures made for community. It is not good for
us to be alone. And even though we, as believers in Christ, always
have His Spirit dwelling in us, I think the Spirit becomes more active
when we join hands and start doing life together!

This is why I love mentorship. Although large-group communities
serve an important role, nothing quite compares to the type of life
change and personal growth one finds in a relationship of two people
specifically committed to one another's growth. It does require
commitment—not only commitment of your time but commitment
of your *self*. Selflessly exploring the life of another person—sharing
fears, hopes, dreams, expectations, struggles, and pains—does not
come naturally to most of us. But the rewards are great if we do.

Relationships are more than the sum of their parts—they take on a life of their own. I want to help you take one person plus one person and see how …

- 1 person + 1 person = 2 people with changed lives
- 1 person + 1 person = 2 people with increased compassion
- 1 person + 1 person = 2 people with new insights, and
- 1 person + 1 person = 2 people experiencing the Spirit of God at work

In healthy mentorship, one plus one really can equal three. This book can help you get there.

The Challenge of Authenticity

Emily knocked apprehensively on the door of the beautiful two-story home nestled in a luxurious suburban community. As a recent college graduate, Emily enjoyed any excuse to escape the cramped apartment she shared with her two roommates, where life seemed so small and yet so empty. *Empty.* That word hung over her like a dark cloud—the perfect description of how she felt lately. She felt lost in the world and desperate for guidance. At the same time, she couldn't escape her compulsive need to put on her "happy face" and pretend she had it all together. She was finally finished with school and entering the real world; she was supposed to be all grown up now, right? But she didn't feel that way inside. That's why she signed up for this mentorship program in the first place. Her church offered it each year, but she had never really paid attention before. Getting paired with a total stranger who would tell her how to live her life sounded like a terrible idea, to be honest. But right now, well, maybe she needed a little advice and direction. If someone actually had answers, she was willing to hear them out this time. She took a deep breath and tried to shove these complicated thoughts aside when she heard the deadbolt click and saw the door swing open.

Martha opened the door with a dramatic flourish and a broad smile, which she hoped would hide the terror and dread she felt in the pit of her stomach. "You must be Emily!" she exclaimed warmly, worried she came across a bit overenthusiastic. She tried to tone it down a bit as she continued. "It's so nice to meet you. Please come inside." Already her head spun with arbitrary anxieties. *Should I offer her a beverage? Should we sit in the kitchen or go to the living room? Am I supposed to have something prepared to talk about? Where do we begin?*

Martha's husband had talked her into becoming a mentor. She never considered herself a mentor type, but she had been on the receiving end of the benefits of mentorship through a relationship with an older woman who had invested in her over the last seven years. Their relationship developed organically, growing deeper over time. Martha knew she could not have endured the last few years without that voice of wisdom and encouragement speaking into her life. God had taken her on an unexpected journey through very difficult experiences recently; but now she finally felt she was getting a stable footing again and was a better—perhaps wiser—person for it. Wasn't it her duty, then, to offer her own wisdom and experience to someone else? But at this very moment, she thought any wisdom or maturity she had must have flown right out through her ears, because all she felt was panicked.

Martha offered Emily a glass of water, and they hesitantly sat down at the kitchen table. "So, tell me about yourself," Martha suggested, hoping the conversation would flow more naturally once they got started.

Emily shared the usual data points about her life, the well-rehearsed introduction people always cover in these initial meeting situations— where she grew up, what she studied in school, where she lived now, and her current job title. In the back of her mind, she couldn't stop the impatient thoughts from pouring through her head. *God, please don't let this be another superficial relationship.* She was looking for someone to help her work through the deep issues in her life, and these surface-level details felt so shallow. Her heart longed to spill forth the real things on her mind—her insecurity about the future, her strained relationship with her father, her fear that God couldn't really love her. But it wasn't safe to talk about those things—not yet. *Building relationships takes time,* she tried to remind herself. She had to play the game—to perform the get-to-know-you dance—and just hope things got better.

Although Emily seemed friendly and willing to share details about her life, Martha sensed she was holding back. More than anything, Martha wanted to create a space where Emily felt safe being herself, but she didn't even know this girl; she had no idea what would put her at ease. In a mentor training session she attended at church, they emphasized the importance of vulnerability. So she decided to try sharing some of her own story. She talked about how she and her husband had been married for over twenty-five years and how he got diagnosed with cancer four years ago. Once she started the story, details poured out almost uncontrollably—how difficult it was hearing the diagnosis, the lengthy battle with chemo, the strain it put on their relationship, and the incredible relief when they learned last year that his cancer was in remission. She wanted to go on, to go deeper and talk more about how much God had taught her through the experience. There were so many lessons she had learned about faith, prayer, trusting His plan, leaning on other people, working through difficult relationships, and understanding who God is and how much He truly loves us. But she wasn't sure which, if any, of these thoughts would be helpful for Emily to hear. She also realized she had been talking for what felt like an eternity but was probably closer to about eight minutes, so she paused for a moment to see if Emily wanted to respond.

"Wow." Emily searched desperately for an appropriate response. "That's an incredible story." And it was. But ... *cancer?* She thought to herself, *I don't know anything about cancer. I can't relate to that experience at all.* She felt nothing but sympathy for everything Martha had been through, and she was grateful that Martha had shared. She did feel like she had gotten to know this woman a little bit better. But the truth was, she had no idea how to respond.

Trying to recover from the awkward moment of silence, Martha went on to share a little bit about the older woman who had walked with her through those dark years and how much it helped having a voice of wisdom and experience to help her see God in the midst of her grief and pain. "That's why I'm doing this mentorship program," she shared. "I know how much of a difference it can make."

As Emily listened to Martha talk about her own mentor, Emily cherished the idea of the kind of relationship Martha described—a woman who knew her deepest struggles and loved her in the midst of them, who wouldn't judge her for her weakness or immaturity, and who was able to offer real insights into her moments of struggle. Emily tried to stifle the bitter thought that kept creeping up in her mind: *this doesn't feel anything like that so far.*

∞

This encounter with Martha and Emily is not a true story—well, not exactly. It is, however, inspired by some encounters with mentorship I've personally had over the years. I've felt both like Emily and like Martha at different times and in different ways. So, let's be real: mentorship can feel *awkward*.

Unfortunately, for many of us, this story represents our worst fears about mentorship, an actual nightmare of judging silence and missed opportunities. These often represent the fears and apprehensions that talk us out of participating in spiritual growth opportunities.

I have good news and bad news for you. The good news is—it's not always like this! I've had experiences with mentorship where a spiritual and emotional bond formed almost instantaneously, and we dove deeply together into the richness of spiritual discipleship. The bad news is—other times it takes more work to push through those initial uncomfortable feelings. But let me tell you, even painfully awkward mentorship relationships can ultimately blossom into deep, beautiful friendships. More importantly, I can honestly say I do not regret a single encounter or attempt with mentoring. Something beautiful came out of every single mentorship relationship I pursued, even the ones that never got off the ground or that eventually fizzled and died. You may never know how deeply you influence someone simply by showing up in a crucial moment.

So please, don't let past negative experiences (or worse yet, just the *fear* of future bad experiences) dissuade you from pursuing the opportunity to invest in one another. I promise, if you just choose to show up, God will use you to enrich the life of another human being. It might not look exactly like the picture you have in your head. (His plan usually looks a bit different than our own ideas.) But it will be great. I guarantee it.

Just remember, we are all only human. We have no magic formula to make us better people. We learn through experiences—good and bad. We grow through trial and error. And we love imperfectly. Still, great beauty lives within our imperfection if we only learn to seek it.

God, teach us to find the beauty in one another's imperfections as you make each one of us more beautiful day by day.

How to Use This Book

Most of us in this twenty-first-century, globalized, westernized world live in societies that (intentionally or not) *discourage* real conversation. Social media makes us well practiced at sharing only the tidbits of information we want others to know, doing so as succinctly as possible. Social networking encourages us to focus on our outward appearances—what we do for a living, where we live, who we live with—rather than engaging with things like character or personal development. We routinely ask and answer questions like, "How are you?" when we know the socially appropriate answer is, "I'm fine. Thanks for asking," even when neither the question nor the answer are sincere. Whether we realize it or not, we become habitually trained as poor conversation partners and even worse companions.

These discussions are intentionally crafted to guide you comfortably through the stages of relationship building—from "nice to meet you" all the way into a thriving mentorship where you can speak into one another's deep fears, struggles, and growth needs. If used on a weekly basis, there are enough conversation guides to last about a year.

Like any tool, this book can be used in a variety of ways, and I encourage you to adapt it to your purposes. However, more than a decade of experience and more than a dozen different types of mentorship relationships have taught me plenty about what works and what doesn't. So, unless you already have a plan, here's what I recommend.

First, consider the type of context and relationships you want to form. I can envision at least three settings in which this tool might prove helpful.

1) One-on-One Mentoring

Whether you pair up through an organized mentorship program or simply seek out another person to speak into your life, this book is *ideally* suited to help take a one-on-one mentorship experience to the next level. I wrote the discussion questions primarily with this context in mind, based on my own experiences and my personal desire to promote deeply authentic interactions between real, flawed human beings who just want to grow and connect. I find that even two people who voluntarily seek out opportunities for deep, purposeful connection still end up feeling awkward and shy when sitting across from one another, trying to figure out what to talk about.

Having a discussion tool like this one helps with three key points of awkwardness:

- It offers probing, thoughtful questions to get the conversation ball rolling.
- It gives you subconscious permission to discuss more intimate issues than normally feel comfortable.
- It provides consistent reminders to integrate scripture and prayer into your interactions.

I recommend trying to tackle one page each time you meet. You can take turns answering all the questions or switch back and forth with each question, but make sure each person gets the opportunity to share all answers and thoughts. Leave time each week to ask, "How can I pray for you this week?" and to share how God responded to your previous prayers. Make notes about both the requests and God's responses in the space provided; I promise you'll be glad to have these records later. Ideally, spend time actually praying together in your meeting, but make sure you continue praying for the other person throughout the week as well. This practice of remembering and praying over another person even when you're not together makes a *huge* difference in the connection you form! Lastly, I recommend you look ahead to the following topic together before you leave your meeting. Certain topics come with special instructions or preparation requirements. Always do your best to spend time contemplating and preparing your answers on your own before you come together to discuss. For best results, *write your answers down.* Seriously. It might feel silly, but it makes sharing your truth so much easier.

2) Small-Group Discussions

Although the word *mentorship* traditionally implies more of a one-on-one relationship, I've seen very similar growth patterns in groups of three or even more. As long as the setting permits sufficient time for all members to share without feeling rushed or distracted, I see no reason why these discussions wouldn't work the same way in small groups as they do one-on-one. For the sake of time constraints, but also personal security and vulnerability issues, I generally would not recommend this book for groups of more than five or six participants. If you have a larger group, consider temporarily splitting into smaller circles during this process of intentionally pursuing growth. Otherwise, feel free to use the same guidelines as for a one-on-one relationship in small-group environments too!

3) Personal Journaling

The discussion topics in this book are primarily intended to help promote relationship and connection as you get to know yourself *and* another person or people. However, you might also benefit from working through the questions individually and focusing on simply getting to know yourself. In this setting, I encourage you to allow ample time to really sit in each of the questions. You might try working through one topic each week but plan to read and journal your thoughts on each question *every day* of that week. I would also encourage you to consistently track your prayer requests and answers to those prayers in the space provided. For best results, I strongly recommend you find an accountability partner who will pray for you during this period and check in on you every once in a while. Growth is hard; it can feel shattering and overwhelming at times. Even if you aren't ready to share that process with another person, it will make a huge difference to remember that you are not alone and that someone cares about who you are and how you are growing.

∞

Once you know the context and/or type of relationship you want to develop, you just need to settle three key decisions:

1. ***Who* will you meet with?**
   If you're connecting through an organized mentorship program (in a church, school, or other organization), this might get decided for you. However, if you get to choose a person (or people) to share this journey with, here are some criteria I recommend:
   a. **Find someone you feel comfortable around.** You don't necessarily need to trust or even know the other person—you can build knowledge, trust, and intimacy through this process—but we all have our own issues and insecurities, and sometimes these cause us to put extra guards up before the relationship even starts. Even if your fears about a person seem arbitrary or unfounded, chances are you'll make better progress if you don't stack the deck against yourself, so to speak, and instead pick someone with whom you can already imagine yourself opening up and sharing honestly.
   b. **Find someone with relevant life experience.** I don't believe mentorship relationships require one older, more

experienced mentor and one younger, less experienced mentee. In fact, I think the best mentoring relationships contain two (or more) people who view each other as peers, regardless of age, status, maturity, or life experience. Still, it helps to find someone who can offer perspectives and observations relevant to you and your current situation. If you want help navigating a specific life event (bereavement, job loss, illness, parenthood, etc.), try to find someone who has some experience with that circumstance. If you want help growing in a specific area (trusting God more fully, being more patient, loving more compassionately, etc.), find someone who exemplifies that trait. Or if you simply want to feel more connected in relationship or community, find someone who shares that desire to connect. You don't *really* need much else in common, but if you share common ground and clarity on what you can offer one another, you will find your relationship grows more naturally and comfortably.

c. **Find someone willing (and able) to commit.** In mentoring (as in all relationships), commitment is key. This type of relationship especially requires deep personal investment and willingness to stick through challenging and potentially painful experiences. Sometimes, even people starting out with the best intentions ultimately back down either when things get difficult or just when life gets complicated. Try to find someone as invested in the process as you are. Establish clear expectations and parameters from the beginning, including a specific commitment timeframe (e.g., commit to meeting at least twice a month for six months, and plan to decide at that point what the new timeframe will look like). One of the biggest threats to all kinds of relationships is lack of clarity about expectations. The best thing you can do for your relationship is clearly define what you will expect from the other person (and yourself) *and* place specific end dates on those expectations so you can both reevaluate periodically as life and circumstances change. There are even some check-up points in this book to make sure you routinely discuss how things are going and what might need to change for the sake of your sanity and relationship.

d. **Don't overthink it!** Sometimes people fall into the trap of thinking good mentorship depends on finding the "right person." Let me burst that bubble right now. There is no right person ideally suited to deal with you and all your issues. We are all just broken, insecure humans who deeply crave love, friendship, and happiness. We all have something to offer one another, and we all have wounds and defenses that sometimes rub up uncomfortably against one another. But we need each other. If you can find another person who meets the criteria already described and decide to pursue relationship, even if the person is not always everything you might desire, I promise you will learn and grow from one another and find yourselves better, more compassionate people in the end.

2) *When* **will you meet?**
One of my favorite leadership coaches, Michael Hyatt, constantly reminds me, "What gets scheduled gets done." I believe nothing better sets up your spiritual growth for success than building it in as a priority in your schedule. Once your partner or group members are committed, work together to establish clear and consistent meeting times. I believe a weekly commitment best promotes trust-building and creates an experience of real involvement in one another's lives. However, finding a routine that feels reasonable and realistic to everyone involved is always better than someone feeling pressured to do more than he or she realistically can.

That said, once you establish your schedule expectations, fill your heart with grace and forgiveness toward the reality that sometimes life will get in the way for one or both of you. Remember the real purpose of your relationship—growing together and supporting one another—and remain willing to adjust less important goals (like consistent meeting times) in favor of the more important objective.

3) *Where* **will you meet?**

This might seem like an unimportant detail, but I've seen environment play a huge role in helping (or hindering) authentic relationships. Ultimately, focus on whatever factors seem most important to you and your partner(s), but here are a few considerations to keep in mind.

   a. **Make it comfortable.** You will already be probing some uncomfortable areas of your life together; don't exacerbate the discomfort through the environment. For me, coffee shops are my happy place, so I do a lot of mentoring there. I've also met people in living rooms, hotel lobbies, restaurants, and even by the poolside over margaritas! Look for a place where you can relax and focus on one another instead of environmental distractions.

   b. **Make it convenient for everyone.** Try to find a location more-or-less convenient for all participants. The more effort required to get there, the more likely someone will end up backing out of the commitment at some point.

   c. **Make it private.** This can be a real trade-off issue—finding somewhere truly private often requires sacrificing comfort or convenience. However, the more private the environment, the more honest people become. My deepest relationships formed in places where we could (and did) end up bawling together, praying over one another, and sharing intimate details that we probably would not have shared if we had gathered in a restaurant or coffee shop instead of behind a closed door. If possible, consider gathering at someone's home (only if kids/spouses/pets, etc. won't be there to distract) or rent a conference room, meeting space, or find a study room at a local library. Look for somewhere soundproof and closed off, so no one feels concerns about being watched or overheard.

By implementing these tips and tricks, you will set yourself up for success and free your mind and heart to focus on the really important aspects of interpersonal growth—honesty and sincerity.

Here are just a few last best practices to keep in mind.

1) Remember, there are no right or wrong answers; just be honest about where you are in your heart and mind.
2) Listen. Listen. Listen. No, seriously, just listen. Most of us need to feel heard so much more than we need answers to our questions.
3) Don't judge. Different does not mean wrong. Wrong does not mean evil. Remember you are both here to experience growth—that means ultimately letting go of certain thought patterns or beliefs. But the only way to get there is to examine those patterns, not condemn them.

Before You Begin

At the start of every journey, you must begin with two essential things in mind: where you are going, and more importantly, why you are going there. Take at least fifteen to twenty minutes to reflect on the following questions *before your first mentorship meeting.* You may choose to share these answers with your partner—or not. But start by *honestly* answering them for yourself.

What made you decide to embark
on this process right now?

What would you like to gain from the experience?

What emotions are you feeling at this point?

What fears or concerns do you have?

In what ways do you think this experience
might help you grow?

Getting to Know You

These first ten sessions focus on helping you explore yourself and one another. Whether you are brand-new acquaintances or already old friends, I think you'll be surprised how little you know about one another (and yourself) as you work through these questions. Before diving into some of your most deeply vulnerable spaces, it's important to build up a level of trust and mutual understanding. Some people with extra doses of self-awareness may easily find answers to these questions; others may need time to process, contemplate, or remember experiences from their past or aspects of their inner world. I encourage you to read and spend a few minutes reflecting on these questions *before* you meet to share them with your partner or group.

Create a safe space to think, self-reflect, and search for honest answers. The goal is not merely to answer the question; the goal is to explore yourself, get to know your partner, and find deeper levels of understanding and compassion. The more you are willing to invest in this exploration, the more you (and your partner) will get out of it.

Heritage

Tell me about the culture you were raised in
(could be family, cultural, racial, or ethnic).

What are some of the core values your cultural
environment contributed to your worldview?

What aspects of your cultural upbringing do you
appreciate? What do you hope to do differently
in your own family and community?

For Further Study:

Numbers 14:18–23, Romans 12:1–3

How has God been speaking to you lately?

_____

_____

_____

_____

How can I pray for you this week?

_____

_____

_____

_____

_____

Favorite Experience

Tell me about one of your favorite experiences—a time when you felt completely yourself.

What aspects of your personality, your skills, or your identity were being used in that experience?

What in your current job, community, or lifestyle makes use of those same aspects of yourself?

For Further Study:

Proverbs 16:1–11, 1 Corinthians 12:4–11

How has God responded to our prayers from last week?

_____

_____

_____

_____

How can I pray for you this week?

_____

_____

_____

_____

_____

_____

_____

Personal Heroes

Tell me about someone who profoundly impacted your life.

What did they do that you want to emulate? What steps are you taking to become more like them in that way?

How can I help you become that kind of person?

For Further Study:

Proverbs 13:14–20, 2 Timothy 1:5–7, 3:10–15

How has God responded to our prayers from last week?

_____

_____

_____

_____

How can I pray for you this week?

_____

_____

_____

_____

_____

_____

_____

_____

Favorite Bible Passage

What is one of your favorite verses,
passages, or stories from scripture?

Why did it have such an impact on you?

What is another favorite and why?

For Further Study:

Psalm 119:9–16, 2 Timothy 3:14–17

How has God responded to our prayers from last week?

_____

_____

_____

_____

How can I pray for you this week?

_____

_____

_____

_____

_____

_____

_____

_____

_____

Needs of the World

What do you consider the most pressing
need in the world today?

What do you consider the most pressing
need in the Church today?

What are you most passionate about
doing to meet these needs?

For Further Study:

Isaiah 58:6–12, Matthew 14:13–21

How has God responded to our prayers from last week?

_____

_____

_____

_____

How can I pray for you this week?

_____

_____

_____

_____

_____

_____

_____

Identity Roles

What are the primary roles you play at this stage of your life? (e.g., wife, mother, son, caregiver, lawyer, manager, volunteer, etc.)

Which of these do you most enjoy?
Which are most challenging?

What roles (whether you currently fill them or not) does your culture value most? What roles do you personally value most?

For Further Study:

Genesis 1:26–28, Colossians 3:17–24

How has God responded to our prayers from last week?

_____

_____

_____

_____

How can I pray for you this week?

_____

_____

_____

_____

_____

Hardships

When you look at your life so far, what stands out as
one of the most difficult times you've endured?

What kinds of doubts and fears did
that experience raise for you?

What helped you work through these struggles?
What are you still wrestling through?

For Further Study:

Job 10:1–22, 42:1–6, James 1:2–4

How has God responded to our prayers from last week?

_____

_____

_____

_____

How can I pray for you this week?

_____

_____

_____

_____

_____

_____

_____

Character of God

When you think about the person and character of
God, what aspects of Him are most real to you?

When you were younger, what was your
picture of God like? How has it changed?

How would you describe your relationship with God
now? How would you like it to change in the future?

For Further Study:

Exodus 33:12–23, Colossians 1:15–20

How has God responded to our prayers from last week?

_____

_____

_____

_____

How can I pray for you this week?

_____

_____

_____

_____

_____

_____

_____

Religious Background

What was your religious upbringing? If you were raised in the church, what denomination or style of worship?

How did your religious experiences impact your view of God?

What is important to you currently about the methods and environments through which you worship God?

For Further Study:

Deuteronomy 10:12–22, Hebrews 10:19–25

How has God responded to our prayers from last week?

_____

_____

_____

_____

How can I pray for you this week?

_____

_____

_____

_____

_____

_____

Mentorship Check-Up

Take a moment to look back over this mentorship experience. What has been your favorite part so far?

What do you notice is different about yourself compared to when you first started?

What do you notice is different about your partner?

(If you have time remaining, flip back through previous pages and revisit some of your favorite questions, or find ones you might answer differently now.)

For Further Study:

Proverbs 27:10, 17, Colossians 3:12–17

How has God responded to our prayers from last week?

_____

_____

_____

How can I pray for you this week?

_____

_____

_____

_____

_____

Digging Deeper

These fifteen sessions focus on digging down past mere understanding toward deeply appreciating one another and thoughtfully speaking into one another's lives. It builds on the knowledge gained in the "Getting to Know You" section, helping you go from *recognizing* who you are to discovering *why* you are that way. What motivates you? What fears and insecurities compel you? What deep longings in your heart are you searching to fulfill?

Always remember that being different does not make someone wrong. We all come from different backgrounds, different life experiences, different personalities and perspectives. These differences influence us in deeper ways than we realize. Frequently, many of us tend to assume others think and operate from the same framework we do. As you peel through the layers of yourself and your partner, you may be surprised to discover things you *don't* share in common. Don't try to change the other person. Appreciate the beautiful uniqueness we have as individuals before God. Strive to understand *the other person's* needs, given their unique history, personality, strengths, and weaknesses.

Christian Testimony

Have you made an intentional decision to surrender your life to Christ as your Savior? If so, tell me about when and why you made that choice. If not, tell me about your journey with God so far.

Have you been baptized as a believer? What is the significance of that decision for you personally?

What does your day-to-day relationship God look like now? What would you like to be different?

For Further Study:

2 Chronicles 7:14, Romans 10:9–13

How has God responded to our prayers from last week?

_____

_____

_____

_____

How can I pray for you this week?

_____

_____

_____

_____

_____

Heroes and Idols

What kind of person do you idolize (in good ways or bad)?
What specific people do you often wish you could be like?

What traits, specifically, draw you to
that person or personality type?

Of those traits, which ones do you actually want to foster
in yourself? Which ones would be unhealthy to emulate?

For Further Study:

Exodus 20:2–6, 1 Corinthians 2:1–5, 4:14–16

How has God responded to our prayers from last week?

_____

_____

_____

_____

How can I pray for you this week?

_____

_____

_____

_____

_____

_____

_____

Accomplishments

What do you consider do be your greatest
accomplishment in life so far?

Tell me about why it was so significant for you.
Did/do others in your life consider it similarly significant?

What do you hope to achieve next?

For Further Study:

Deuteronomy 8:11–18, Ephesians 2:8–10

How has God responded to our prayers from last week?

_____

_____

_____

_____

How can I pray for you this week?

_____

_____

_____

_____

_____

_____

_____

_____

Your Story—Person #1

Tell me, briefly, the story of your life.

Try to hit major sections, formative experiences, and key turning points. Feel free to reflect on the emotions experienced during significant stages and lessons learned that impacted your worldview or future behaviors.

After sharing, the listener should respond to these questions:

- What did you hear?
- What did you relate to?
- How can you encourage this person?

(Plan to spend two or more sessions on this activity, so you each get time to share. Two copies of this page are provided—one for each person's story.)

For Further Study:

Psalm 136, Revelation 12:10–11

How has God responded to our prayers from last week?

_____

_____

_____

How can I pray for you this week?

_____

_____

_____

Your Story—Person #2

Tell me, briefly, the story of your life.

Try to hit major sections, formative experiences, and key turning points. Feel free to reflect on the emotions experienced during significant stages and lessons learned that impacted your worldview or future behaviors.

After sharing, the listener should respond to these questions:

- What did you hear?
- What did you relate to?
- How can you encourage this person?

(Plan to spend two or more sessions on this activity, so you each get time to share. Two copies of this page are provided—one for each person's story.)

For Further Study:

Psalm 136, Revelation 12:10–11

How has God responded to our prayers from last week?

_____

_____

_____

How can I pray for you this week?

_____

_____

Reflecting on Your Stories

In light of your story (in the previous sessions),
how do you see God used your experiences
to prepare you to better love others?

What have you learned about yourself that you
want to remember in the future? How do you
think it might change future decisions?

What parts of your story still feel unfinished?
What chapters do you think are closed,
and which ones are still unfolding?

For Further Study:

Psalm 119:89–96, Philippians 1:3–6

How has God responded to our prayers from last week?

_____

_____

_____

_____

How can I pray for you this week?

_____

_____

_____

_____

_____

Uniqueness

Tell me something about yourself that
people probably would not expect.

What do you consider yourself to be above average at?
What do you enjoy more than anything else?

What do people often praise you or
compliment you for? Do you agree with their
assessments of yourself? Why or why not?

For Further Study:

Psalm 139:1–16, Romans 12:3–8

How has God responded to our prayers from last week?

_____

_____

_____

_____

How can I pray for you this week?

_____

_____

_____

_____

_____

_____

_____

Decisions

What key decisions in your life have
led you where you are today?

If you could go back, knowing what you know now,
would you make the same decision(s) again?

Do you tend to approach life as though you have a
specific destiny or as though you choose your destiny?

For Further Study:

Joshua 24:15, Ephesians 1:3–6

How has God responded to our prayers from last week?

_____

_____

_____

_____

How can I pray for you this week?

_____

_____

_____

_____

_____

_____

_____

Family Relationships

How would you describe your relationship
with your family? How has the way you relate
changed over the course of your life?

How were discipline and criticism handled in your family
growing up? How did the family show praise and affection?

How do you think your family dynamic has impacted
your view of God or the way you relate to Him?

For Further Study:

Exodus 20:12, Matthew 10:34–39

How has God responded to our prayers from last week?

_____

_____

_____

_____

How can I pray for you this week?

_____

_____

_____

_____

_____

_____

Mentorship Check-Up

Take a moment to look back over this mentorship experience. What has challenged you about this process?

What do you most appreciate about your partner(s) so far?

Is there anything you would prefer to change about how you both approach your relationship and/or time together?

(If you have time remaining, flip back through previous pages and revisit some of your favorite questions, or find ones you might answer differently now.)

For Further Study:

Ecclesiastes 4:8–12, Acts 2:42–47

How has God responded to our prayers from last week?

_____

_____

_____

_____

How can I pray for you this week?

_____

_____

_____

_____

_____

_____

Security

What things cause you to feel more secure in life (money, power, friendships, home life, career, time alone, etc.)?

What enables you to feel safe and be vulnerable around other people? What causes you to shut down?

What aspects of your desire for personal security bring glory to God? What might He want you to let go of?

For Further Study:

Psalm 20, 1 John 2:15–17

How has God responded to our prayers from last week?

_____

_____

_____

_____

How can I pray for you this week?

_____

_____

_____

_____

_____

_____

_____

Personality and Self-Concept

How would you describe yourself?
What key features distinguish you from others?

How might your unique traits challenge your
ability to love others well? How might they
equip you to love people better?

How might your view of yourself affect
your relationship with God?

For Further Study:

Exodus 3:11–15, 4:10–13, Matthew 16:13–20

How has God responded to our prayers from last week?

_____

_____

_____

_____

How can I pray for you this week?

_____

_____

_____

_____

_____

_____

Past Wounds

Tell me about a time when you experienced
woundedness, oppression, or betrayal.

How did that experience (or others like it) shape
your view of the world and your view of yourself?

What has helped you heal from past wounds like this?
What healing still needs to take place in your life?

For Further Study:

Psalm 6, Matthew 5:1–12

How has God responded to our prayers from last week?

_____

_____

_____

_____

How can I pray for you this week?

_____

_____

_____

_____

_____

_____

_____

_____

Sin

How was sin treated and discussed in your upbringing?

How would you describe your current attitude toward sin?

How have your perspectives on sin changed as
you have grown in your relationship with God?

For Further Study:

Genesis 6:5–8, Romans 5:6–21

How has God responded to our prayers from last week?

_____

_____

_____

_____

How can I pray for you this week?

_____

_____

_____

_____

_____

_____

_____

_____

_____

Spiritual Growth

As you look back on your spiritual journey, what formulaic approaches to spiritual growth have you been exposed to?

What did you find helpful about these approaches? What was not helpful?

What is an area of growth God is working on in you in this season?

For Further Study:

Psalm 119:33–40, 1 Peter 2:1–5

How has God responded to our prayers from last week?

_____

_____

_____

_____

How can I pray for you this week?

_____

_____

_____

_____

_____

_____

_____

Growing Together

These fifteen sessions will push you a bit out of your comfort zone into a place of openness and vulnerability. Get ready to confront things such as sin struggles, deep-seated fears, and the secrets you may try to hide. If you're working through these questions weekly, you should be about six to seven months into your mentorship relationship. Congratulations! Hopefully, this time, and your intentional use of it, has helped develop trust and compassion toward one another. You may not agree about everything—that's okay. You can still love one another exactly where you are.

If your journey has been rocky so far (it happens, it's okay!) and you don't feel ready for this level of vulnerability yet, consider taking a short break from this book. Spend a few weeks just praying together, lifting the other person up to God. If there are conflicts between you, set aside time to work through them. If it would be helpful, invite a third party in to mediate, share wisdom, or facilitate reconciliation. *Don't move on pretending everything is okay.* (You can also check out some of the Recommended Resources at the back of this book for ideas on how to work through specific issues and continue building trust.)

Be prepared to bear one another's burdens. You cannot fix your partner's problems. But you can stand beside one another and help your partner feel less alone. Try to remind each other of the hope we have as believers, the freedom Christ bought for us on the cross, and the enduring faithfulness of God.

Spiritual Gifts

Have you identified your own spiritual gifts?
(If not, consider taking an assessment to learn
what they are. Some Recommended Resources
are listed in the back of this book.)

How have you been able to use your gift(s) to glorify God?

Why do you think spiritual gifts matter in the
church and in the functioning of a society?

For Further Study:

Exodus 31:1–11, 1 Corinthians 12:4–12

How has God responded to our prayers from last week?

_____

_____

_____

_____

How can I pray for you this week?

_____

_____

_____

_____

_____

_____

Faith and Doubt

Carefully consider the following statements:

"God loves me just the way I am."

"I don't need to earn God's favor."

"God wants to give me good gifts."

"I know I am secure in my salvation."

"God wants to share Himself with me."

Which statement do you have the hardest
time trusting and living in that belief? Why is
it difficult for you to believe that truth?

Which statement do you believe
most? Why is that one easier?

For Further Study:

Psalm 33:4–5, Hebrews 12:1–2

How has God responded to our prayers from last week?

_____

_____

_____

_____

How can I pray for you this week?

_____

_____

_____

_____

Prayer

What does your prayer life look like?
How often do you approach God in prayer?

What do you enjoy about prayer?
What do you struggle with?

What kinds of prayer do you see practiced in scripture?
What new approaches to prayer would
you like to integrate in your life?

For Further Study:

2 Chronicles 7:13–16, Matthew 6:5–15

How has God responded to our prayers from last week?

_____

_____

_____

_____

How can I pray for you this week?

_____

_____

_____

_____

_____

_____

_____

The Triune God

What do you think it means to say God is
one God who exists in three persons?

Of the three persons, Father, Son, and Holy
Spirit, to which do you feel closest? To whom
do you typically address your prayers?

What might we learn about God's character from the fact
that He reveals Himself in these three distinct persons?

For Further Study:

Deuteronomy 6:4–5, John 14:16–17, 25–26

How has God responded to our prayers from last week?

_____

_____

_____

_____

How can I pray for you this week?

_____

_____

_____

_____

_____

_____

Mentorship Check-Up

Take a moment to look back over this
mentorship experience. What has made
the biggest impact on your life?

What do you most appreciate about your partner
now, in light of what you're learning about them?

Is there anything you would prefer to change about how
you both approach your relationship and/or time together?

*(If you have time remaining, flip back through previous
pages and revisit some of your favorite questions, or
find ones you might answer differently now.)*

For Further Study:

Psalm 1, Matthew 5:23–25

How has God responded to our prayers from last week?

_____

_____

_____

_____

How can I pray for you this week?

_____

_____

_____

_____

Seven Deadly Sins

Historically, the seven deadly sins are pride, greed, lust, envy, gluttony, wrath, and sloth. Describe what you think each one means.

Which do you find yourself most inclined toward in your daily life?

What is one sin you used to struggle with that no longer causes you the same struggle?

For Further Study:

Psalm 51:1–6, Matthew 5:29–30

How has God responded to our prayers from last week?

_____

_____

_____

_____

How can I pray for you this week?

_____

_____

_____

_____

_____

_____

_____

Relationships

What are some relationships in which you are struggling to love in a Christ-like way?

What are some relationships where you find yourself easily able to love selflessly?

What do you learn about your own character from the way you interact in relationships with others?

For Further Study:

Leviticus 19:11–17, John 13:34–35

How has God responded to our prayers from last week?

_____

_____

_____

_____

How can I pray for you this week?

_____

_____

_____

_____

_____

_____

_____

_____

The Holy Spirit

What do you understand the role and function
of the Holy Spirit to be in your own life?
Do you experience Him regularly?

What do you think it means to "walk
by the Spirit" (Galatians 5:16)?

What specific things in your daily life might look different
if you were walking more according to the Spirit?

For Further Study:

2 Samuel 23:2, John 14:16–17, 25–26

How has God responded to our prayers from last week?

_____

_____

_____

_____

How can I pray for you this week?

_____

_____

_____

_____

_____

_____

Fruit of the Spirit

The Spirit helps to correct sin patterns, replacing them with Spirit-filled patterns instead. How do you see the Spirit's work producing "fruit" (healthy patterns) in your life now?

The classic "fruit of the spirit" are love, joy, peace, patience, kindness, goodness, faith, gentleness, self-control. Which three do you think are most evident in you to others? Which two do you think God might be working on most in you lately?

Which fruits do you see most evident in your mentorship partner?

For Further Study:

Psalm 5:4–12, Galatians 5:16–25

How has God responded to our prayers from last week?

_____

_____

_____

_____

How can I pray for you this week?

_____

_____

_____

_____

Voice of God

How have you seen God communicate to you in big moments? Do you see Him guiding your decisions and life changes? How do you discern His voice?

How does God communicate with you in smaller day-to-day activities? Do you consult Him about small things? Why or why not?

How do you wish God spoke to you differently? Why do you think He doesn't speak in that way?

For Further Study:

1 Kings 19:9–18, Acts 9:1–19.

How has God responded to our prayers from last week?

_____

_____

_____

_____

How can I pray for you this week?

_____

_____

_____

_____

_____

Exercise: Spiritual Disciplines

Spiritual disciplines help us retrain our habits and reform our focus. They come in all shapes and sizes, but for now, *choose a spiritual discipline from the following list to practice for one week.*

Solitude, Silence, Fasting, Bible Reading, Worship, Prayer, Journaling, Service, Generosity Try to choose one that is not already part of your usual activities

How did God use this week to reveal Himself to you? What did you learn about yourself through the process?

(For more great info on spiritual disciplines, check out some of the Recommended Resources at the back of this book.)

For Further Study:

Psalm 18:30–34, 1 Timothy 4:7–10

How has God responded to our prayers from last week?

_____

_____

_____

_____

How can I pray for you this week?

_____

_____

_____

_____

Relationship with God

Describe what you wish your relationship with God looked like. Be really honest. Would He give you all your desires? Would He talk to you every day? Would He answer all your questions? How would He interact with you in this "ideal" scenario?

In what ways does this image of your relationship represent a healthy goal? In what ways might the vision need to change?

How do you think God wishes your relationship looked different?

For Further Study:

Deuteronomy 11:18–25, 1 John 1:5–9

How has God responded to our prayers from last week?

_____

_____

_____

_____

How can I pray for you this week?

_____

_____

_____

_____

Conflict

How do you deal with conflict? Do you try to avoid it, or do you tackle it head on? What about you makes you choose that strategy?

Do you think people would describe you as a good conflict resolver or someone who escalates conflict? How do you feel about this?

What do you appreciate in yourself about how you handle tough situations? What would you like to change or grow?

For Further Study:

Proverbs 15:1, 27:6, Colossians 3:12–17

How has God responded to our prayers from last week?

_____

_____

_____

_____

How can I pray for you this week?

_____

_____

_____

_____

_____

_____

Calling

What do you think it means to be "called" by God?
(Consider Deut. 28:10, Rom. 8:28, 11:29,
2 Tim. 1:9, and 2 Pet. 1:10.)

What do you believe God has called you to
do—in the past, present, or future? How
have you responded to that call?

What holds you back from pursuing the
things you are called to do?

For Further Study:

Isaiah 41:8–10, 42:5–7, 2 Peter 1:3–11

How has God responded to our prayers from last week?

_____

_____

_____

_____

How can I pray for you this week?

_____

_____

_____

_____

_____

_____

Character

How do you think God would describe you? What would stand out most to Him about who you are?

How do you think other people would describe you? Would they see the same things God does? What would be different about their perspectives of you?

Whose opinions do you want to change more—God's view of you or other people's view of you? What do you want to change and why?

For Further Study:

Psalm 139:1–16, 1 John 3:18–24

How has God responded to our prayers from last week?

_____

_____

_____

_____

How can I pray for you this week?

_____

_____

_____

_____

_____

_____

Wrestling with the World

The last ten sessions consider real issues and pain points you will face in the world. These questions should challenge you to confront your own beliefs and opinions about these issues and to run them thoughtfully through the filters of scripture and spiritual growth. Because of the sensitive nature of many of these topics, you may need some extra grace and compassion toward one another as you discuss them together.

Please remember, it is not important that you agree on these topics. All of us are simply walking through life making judgments and decisions as best we can. This is a great opportunity to practice identifying and articulating your own beliefs and to sharpen them against the insights of another person. However, you may need to be comfortable simply agreeing to disagree at the end of some sessions, and that's okay!

Spiritual Realm

What do you currently believe about the unseen dynamics of this world? Do you believe in angels? Demons? Ghosts? Spirits? Fairies?

How did you arrive at your current belief system? Are you open to the possibility of things you don't see or can't understand? Why or why not?

How do you think these beliefs impact your view of God?

For Further Study:

1 Samuel 28:1–21, Ephesians 6:12–13

How has God responded to our prayers from last week?

_____

_____

_____

_____

How can I pray for you this week?

_____

_____

_____

_____

_____

_____

_____

The Afterlife

What significant people in your life have died? How old were you? How did these experiences impact you at the time? How do they affect you still?

When you think of the afterlife, what do you picture? What about those images brings you comfort? What makes you uncomfortable?

How well does your image of the afterlife line up with scripture?

For Further Study:

Job 38:1–4, 16–24, 1 Thessalonians 4:13–18

How has God responded to our prayers from last week?

_____

_____

_____

_____

How can I pray for you this week?

_____

_____

_____

_____

_____

_____

Injustice

What do you perceive as the greatest source/
example of injustice in the world today? (Try to
refrain from assigning blame or proposing solutions;
instead focus on what grips your heart.)

What makes you passionate about this topic
in particular? Are there personal experiences
that help you identify with this issue?

What are you doing to impact this issue?
What do you wish you could do?

For Further Study:

Proverbs 3:27–35, James 2:8–18

How has God responded to our prayers from last week?

_____

_____

_____

_____

How can I pray for you this week?

_____

_____

_____

_____

_____

Discrimination

In what ways have you felt like a minority
in different environments? Describe the
experience. How did others treat you?

In what ways do you belong to a majority group in
your life? How do you think about those who don't "fit
the mold" in those contexts? Have you ever treated
someone badly because he or she was different?

Why do you think these experiences hurt so much?

For Further Study:

Leviticus 19:33–37, Luke 10:29–37

How has God responded to our prayers from last week?

_____

_____

_____

_____

How can I pray for you this week?

_____

_____

_____

_____

_____

Mentorship Check-Up

Take a moment to look back over this
mentorship experience. In what areas have
you experienced the most healing?

What new things have you come to appreciate about
your partner, as you've gotten closer to them?

Is there anything you need to address about how you
both approach your relationship and/or time together?

*(If you have time remaining, flip back through previous
pages and revisit some of your favorite questions, or
find ones you might answer differently now.)*

For Further Study:

Proverbs 12:22–26, Philippians 4:10–19

How has God responded to our prayers from last week?

_____

_____

_____

_____

How can I pray for you this week?

_____

_____

_____

_____

Gender Roles

Do you think God created men and women fundamentally differently or fundamentally the same?

Beyond anatomy, what main differences do you observe between masculinity and femininity? Do you think these differences are socially constructed or part of God's design or both? Why?

In what ways have you been treated differently because of your gender? What do you like or dislike about these differences?

For Further Study:

Genesis 2:4–24, 1 Corinthians 11:8–16

How has God responded to our prayers from last week?

_____

_____

_____

_____

How can I pray for you this week?

_____

_____

_____

_____

_____

_____

Society and Government

What do you think is the main purpose of a government or ruler? What responsibilities does it/he or she have? What can get in the way of its/hers or his proper functioning?

What do you appreciate about the type of government you currently live under? What concerns do you have about it?

How do you think Christians should integrate social responsibility and submission to God's authority?

For Further Study:

1 Samuel 8:4–22, Matthew 22:15–22

How has God responded to our prayers from last week?

_____

_____

_____

_____

How can I pray for you this week?

_____

_____

_____

_____

_____

_____

_____

Sexual Behavior

Why do you think God created sex? What is its primary purpose? What other purposes might it have?

How have people misused the gift of sexuality through the history of humankind? What ways do we use sex to seek our own glory instead of God's?

What do you think a healthy, God-honoring sexual relationship should look like? Have you experienced this kind of relationship?

For Further Study:

Leviticus 18:1–24, 1 Corinthians 5:9–13, 6:12–20.

How has God responded to our prayers from last week?

_____

_____

_____

How can I pray for you this week?

_____

_____

_____

_____

_____

_____

_____

Exercise: Dream for Each Other

Congratulations!
By now, you've spent nearly a year (or more)
getting to know each other and participating in
God's work in one another's lives. Now it's time
to see how deeply you really know each other.

This week, spend some time dreaming big *for your partner.* Imagine what their best life might be like. Where would they live? What would their family be like? What career and/or ministry work would they be doing?

Share your ideas/dreams together. Do not respond right away to what is shared. You may ask clarifying questions or explore why they would suggest those ideas, but do not contradict or add to the things your partner shares. Just listen with an open mind and consider how God might be speaking.

For Further Study:

Proverbs 16:1–9, Ephesians 3:20–21

How has God responded to our prayers from last week?

_____

_____

_____

How can I pray for you this week?

_____

_____

Future Plans

When you were young, what did you want to be when you grew up? Why do you think that appealed to you?

Where do you see yourself five years from now? Where do you want to live? What do you want to be doing? Who do you want to be with?

What specific steps would you need to start taking now to get from where you are now to where you want to be?

For Further Study:

Psalm 127:1–2, Philippians 1:6

How has God responded to our prayers from last week?

_____

_____

_____

_____

How can I pray for you this week?

_____

_____

_____

_____

_____

_____

Endings and Beginnings

I hope you know that whoever you are, wherever you are, I have prayed for you. I pray that this book serves your pursuit to find meaningful relationships with other people. I pray you find yourself experiencing deeper levels of connection and more sincere love toward the people in your life.

I hope you will take the opportunity to stop and recognize what you have accomplished so far. Relationships take hard work. They require time, energy, and endless amounts of patience and perseverance. The journey of human relationships and Christian fellowship never ends, but you should stop and enjoy the landmarks when you find them.

Take some time to celebrate with your partner. Get dressed up and go to a fancy dinner. Take a mini-vacation together. Go to a sporting event, a concert, an opera—whatever makes you both feel appreciated. Just take time to recognize the value of what you have invested.

Whether this is the start of a lifelong relationship or a one-time season in your life, make a point to thank your partner for the ways he or she has impacted you. The time you invested in one another has changed you both forever. I encourage you to ask these questions together:

How has our time together impacted you?

If you could go back to the beginning and do it over again, would you do anything differently?

How can I pray for God to bless you in
the next season of your life?

Recommended Resources

There are many wonderful resources available on these crucial topics, but each of these resources made a special impact on me and may help you dig deeper into the following topics.

On Mentoring

Mentor 101 **by John C. Maxwell**
An accessible overview describing the purpose and best practices for mentoring within Christian contexts.

Organic Mentoring **by Sue Edwards and Barbara Neumann**
A penetrating and engaging look at what mentoring can and should look like in the modern era, especially in light of generational differences among older and younger women.

The Coaching Habit **by Michael Bungay Stanier**
Describes the role of a mentor/coach in a secular leadership context, with a heavy focus on what it looks like to listen well and engage with another person.

On Personal Assessment Tools

StrengthsFinder 2.0 by Tom Rath

A highly detailed personal analysis with online assessment test to determine what unique strengths set you apart in your work and daily lifestyle.

www.16personalities.com

A great online resource with a free assessment test based on the Myers-Briggs Temperament Inventory.

The Road Back to You by Ian Morgan Cron and Suzanne Stabile

An introductory primer on the complex system of personal assessment known as the "Enneagram," helping readers understand themselves better by identifying core fears, insecurities, and motivations.

On Spiritual Growth

Messy Spirituality **by Michael Yaconelli**
An honest reminder of what it looks like to be human, to receive grace, and to grow spiritually as real, messy people.

Mere Christianity **by C. S. Lewis**
A true classic and a must-read for believers. Lewis takes a probing look at the most essential doctrines of the Christian faith and why they define us a Christians.

Renovation of the Heart **by Dallas Willard**
A longstanding source of wisdom, describing the nature of spiritual growth and what it looks like to take on the character of Christ in our hearts and lives.

The Pursuit of God **by A. W. Tozer**
Another classic, which gazes deeply into the character of God, the nature of man, and the incomprehensible process by which we seek to understand and develop intimacy with Him.

On Spiritual Disciplines

The Spirit of the Disciplines **by Dallas Willard**

One of the best depictions I've found of the true purpose behind practicing specific disciplines in the process of growing faith and love toward God. Also contains detailed lists and descriptions of disciplines worth practicing.

With Christ in the School of Prayer **by Andrew Murray**

A dense but powerful short book on how to take the practice of prayer to a deeper level and understand better how Christ wants us to pray.

On Dealing with Sin

The Grace Awakening **by Charles R. Swindoll**
A potent, heart-piercing reminder of the power and efficacy of God's grace in our lives and spiritual development.

The Screwtape Letters **by C. S. Lewis**
A gripping fictional depiction of the real and active demonic enemies who seek to disarm and destroy believers through subtle manipulations toward sinful patterns of living.

Boundaries **by Henry Cloud and John Townsend**
A very practical and systematic examination of the psychological and habitual behaviors and tendencies we battle as we try to become better, more God-honoring people.

On Spiritual Gifts

www.Gifts.ChurchGrowth.org
Offers a detailed and inexpensive online assessment to determine your spiritual gifts and understand what they mean and how to apply them.

Living Your Strengths **by Albert Winseman, Don Clifton, et al.**
From one of the creators of "StrengthsFinder 2.0" comes a similar assessment tool geared specifically at finding your spiritual superpowers and how to use them to God's glory.

Courage and Calling **by Gordon T. Smith**
A beautifully written exhortation to find your place in God's kingdom and work by discovering who you are and how you are best suited to serve God courageously.

About the Author

Alicia is a life-long student of human nature and multi-passionate author and entrepreneur. She holds a B.A. in Humanities, Literature, and Philosophy from Biola University and a M.A. in Christian Education and Leadership from Dallas Theological Seminary. After more than 15 years of teaching and serving in the evangelical church, she is deeply invested in helping believers develop their relationship with God and reach their fullest potential as human beings through establishing healthy relationships with oneself and others.

Printed in the United States
By Bookmasters